A TRUE BOOK™

Dr. Mae Jemison and 100 Year Starship™

Journey Through Our Solar System

DR. MAE JEMISON
AND DANA MEACHEN RAU

Children's Press®
An Imprint of Scholastic Inc.
New York   Toronto   London   Auckland   Sydney
Mexico City   New Delhi   Hong Kong
Danbury, Connecticut

Library of Congress Cataloging-in-Publication Data

Jemison, Mae, 1956–
  Journey through our solar system/by Mae Jemison and Dana Meachen Rau.
     p. cm. — (A true book)
  Includes bibliographical references and index.
  ISBN 978-0-531-25501-8 (library binding) — ISBN 978-0-531-24061-8 (pbk.)
1. Solar system—Juvenile literature. 2. Outer space—Exploration—Juvenile literature.
3. Space probes—Juvenile literature. I. Rau, Dana Meachen, 1971– II. Title. III. Series: True book.
  QB501.3.J45 2013
   523.2—dc23   2012035789

© 2013 Scholastic Inc.

All rights reserved. Published in 2013 by Children's Press, an imprint of Scholastic Inc.
Printed in the United States of America 113
SCHOLASTIC, CHILDREN'S PRESS, A TRUE BOOK™, and associated logos are trademarks and/or
registered trademarks of Scholastic Inc.
1 2 3 4 5 6 7 8 9 10 R 22 21 20 19 18 17 16 15 14 13

Front cover: Artist's illustration of the proposed *Jupiter Icy Moons Orbiter* probe
Back cover: Our solar system

Find the Truth!

Everything you are about to read is true *except* for one of the sentences on this page.

Which one is **TRUE**?

T or F Besides Earth, there is water in at least two other places in our solar system.

T or F No place in our solar system, other than Earth, could ever have supported life.

Find the answers in this book.

Contents

1 The Solar Neighborhood

What makes up our solar system? 7

2 Observing the Skies

How do scientists learn about our solar system? . . . 13

3 Exploring the Inner Solar System

What have NASA probes taught us
about the inner solar system? 21

THE **BIG** TRUTH!

NASA Probe Missions

What probes have explored
our solar system? 30

Curiosity landed
on Mars in 2012.

4 Exploring the Outer Solar System

What have NASA probes taught us about
the outer solar system? **33**

5 The Journey Continues

How will scientists explore farther than before? . . . **41**

True Statistics **44**

Resources **45**

Important Words **46**

Index **47**

About the Authors **48**

For a long time, most
people did not believe the
planets circled the sun.

Planets and other objects orbit around a central star— our sun.

CHAPTER 1

The Solar Neighborhood

The sun is our source of light and heat. This bright ball in the sky may not seem very big, but it is the largest object in our solar system. Because the sun is so large, it has a lot of gravity. All of the planets, dwarf planets, asteroids, comets, and dust that orbit the sun—and all the space between—make up our solar system. The sun's gravity holds it all together.

The sun is the size of 1.3 million Earths.

Inner Solar System

Eight planets **revolve** around the sun in oval-shaped paths. The four planets closest to the sun are called the rocky planets. They make up the inner solar system. These planets are relatively small compared to the sun, and are made mostly of iron and rock. They include Mercury, Venus, Earth, and Mars. Earth's distance from the sun gives it just the right amount of heat and light to support life.

Our solar system is more than 90 billion miles (145 billion kilometers) wide.

OUR SOLAR SYSTEM

Mercury

Venus

Earth

Mars

Jupiter

Outer Solar System

The planets of the outer solar system include Jupiter, Saturn, Uranus, and Neptune. These planets are much larger than the rocky inner planets. They are made completely of gas and have no solid surfaces. Scientists call them gas giants.

Dwarf planets are smaller than all the other planets. Pluto, once considered the ninth planet, is now called a dwarf planet. Ceres is a dwarf planet that orbits between Mars and Jupiter. Eris orbits beyond Neptune.

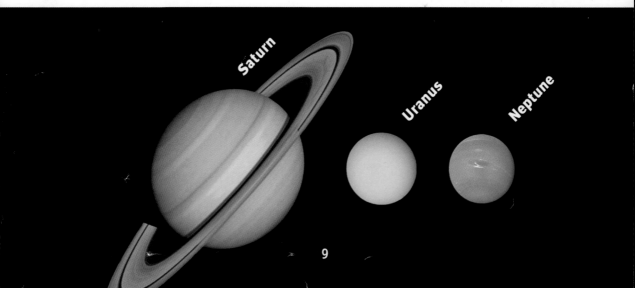

Several meteors might enter Earth's atmosphere in a short amount of time, creating a meteor shower.

Asteroids and Comets

Smaller objects also orbit the sun. Asteroids are chunks of metal and rock. Many are found in the asteroid belt, a ring of asteroids that lies between the orbits of Mars and Jupiter. Meteors are chunks of rock that enter Earth's **atmosphere**. Most meteors burn up as they travel through the atmosphere. When a meteor reaches Earth, it is called a meteorite.

Comets are mostly made of frozen gas, rock, and dust. Their orbits are very **elliptical**, bringing them close to the sun and then far away. Short-period comets may start in the Kuiper Belt, beyond Neptune. These comets take less than 200 years to orbit the sun. Long-period comets take up to 20 million years to orbit. They may start in the Oort Cloud, an area scientists believe exists in the outer reaches of our solar system.

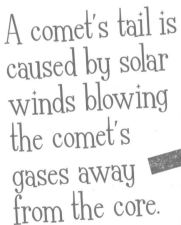

A comet's tail is caused by solar winds blowing the comet's gases away from the core.

11

Solar means having to do with the sun.

In Europe in the 1500s, Nicolaus Copernicus helped popularize the concept of a sun-centered system.

CHAPTER 2

Observing the Skies

Thousands of years ago, astronomers around the world, from China to Egypt to South America, knew the stars and the paths of most planets. Most civilizations believed Earth was the center of this universe. But in 300 BCE, Aristarchus of Samos wrote that Earth and the planets circle the sun, and the sun is a star like other stars. Few people accepted this until 1543 CE, when Nicolaus Copernicus again proposed a sun-centered system. This idea is the basis for modern astronomy.

A Closer Look

Starting in the 1600s, scientists used **telescopes** to make closer observations. Before, the planets Mercury, Venus, Mars, Jupiter, and Saturn had been observed by eye. Comets were only seen when their orbits brought them close to the sun. Telescopes led to the discovery of Uranus, Neptune, Pluto, and many asteroids, comets, and moons. Today, telescopes may be small and handheld, or part of large observatories on Earth. But telescopes have the best vision when they are in space!

Space Observation Timeline

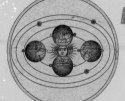

300 BCE
Aristarchus of Samos proposes that Earth and the planets orbit the sun.

1543 CE
Nicolaus Copernicus proposes a sun-centered system.

1610
Galileo uses a telescope to discover moons around Jupiter.

Hubble Space Telescope

Launched by the National Aeronautics and Space Administration (NASA) in 1990, the Hubble Space Telescope (HST) has helped scientists observe even more objects in our solar system and beyond. The HST orbits Earth. It does not have to look through the atmosphere, so it gets a much clearer view of outer space. The HST has shown scientists many amazing images, such as distant galaxies and the birth of stars.

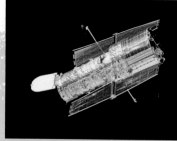

1831
The first ground-based observatory is constructed at the University of North Carolina.

1958
The first U.S. spacecraft, *Explorer 1*, is launched; NASA is created.

1990
NASA launches the Hubble Space Telescope.

Space Probes

Observing an object up close is one of the best ways to learn more about it. But objects in space are too far away for scientists to visit. So engineers and scientists develop spacecraft that can be launched into space to gather information. These **probes** send data back to Earth for scientists to study.

Scientists use rockets to send probes and other spacecraft into space.

16

The *Galileo* probe began orbiting Jupiter in 1995.

Some probes make a one-way trip into space. Others return to Earth with samples.

Flyby probes travel past one or more space objects. Orbiting probes spend more time studying a single object as they orbit it. The goal of an atmospheric probe is to collect data as it drops through a planet's or moon's atmosphere. A lander lands on the surface of that planet or object. A rover is a wheeled probe that can explore the surface over a larger area.

Pioneers 6 through *9* (resembling the probe pictured at the top) were sent to the sun. *Pioneers 10* and *11* (second from top) were sent to the outer solar system. *Pioneers 12* and *13* (bottom two) were sent to Venus.

CHAPTER 3

Exploring the Inner Solar System

The National Aeronautics and Space Administration (NASA) named the earliest space probe mission to the sun *Pioneer*. The word *pioneer* means a person who is the first to explore a new area. The sun is the center of our solar system. Learning more about our star would help scientists learn more about the solar system as a whole.

The Pioneer Project included several different probes.

Observing the Sun

On December 16, 1965, *Pioneer 6* was launched into orbit around the sun. In the three following years, NASA sent up *Pioneers 7, 8,* and *9*. Together, the four probes acted like weather stations around the sun. This helped scientists understand and predict occurrences such as solar storms. The *Pioneer* probes were designed to last about six months. They ended up gathering information for NASA scientists for more than 30 years.

Solar storms can result in huge flares of extra energy.

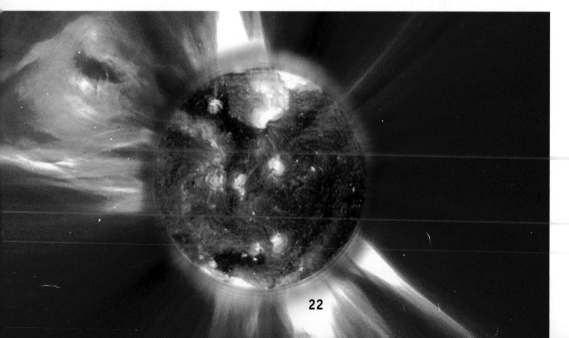

Genesis crash-landed because its parachute did not open.

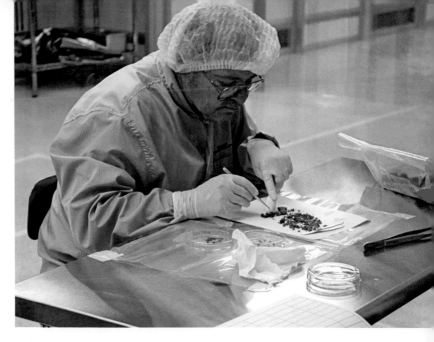

Dr. Don Burnett studies samples of material recovered from *Genesis*.

Ulysses gave scientists a new view of the sun. It was the first probe to study the sun's **poles**. *Ulysses* made three orbits around the sun and gathered data over 18 years. *Genesis* observed solar wind. Solar wind is made up of particles pushed out from the sun. *Genesis* gathered samples and then returned to Earth, landing in the Utah desert. Scientists at the Johnson Space Center in Houston, Texas, are studying these particles.

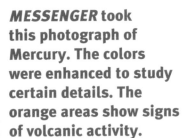

MESSENGER took this photograph of Mercury. The colors were enhanced to study certain details. The orange areas show signs of volcanic activity.

Observing Mercury

The *Mariner 10* probe made a flyby of Mercury, the closest planet to the sun. Its photographs revealed that our smallest planet is covered in craters and ridges, much like our moon. *MESSENGER*, an orbiter probe, entered a path around Mercury in 2011. Already, *MESSENGER* is **transmitting** new information. Images show **evidence** of volcanoes in Mercury's past. *MESSENGER's* goal is to map the entire planet and gather data on its surface, interior, and atmosphere.

Observing Venus

NASA made some interesting discoveries when the *Mariner 2* probe flew by Venus. The probe measured hot surface temperatures of at least 797 degrees Fahrenheit (425 degrees Celsius) and a thick deadly atmosphere containing sulfur. *Magellan* mapped the planet using a special type of **radar** that could see through the clouds. *Magellan* gathered information about the atmosphere before it crashed on Venus's surface.

Magellan was the first planetary probe launched from a space shuttle.

Magellan was able to see through Venus's thick clouds (left) to its rocky surface (right).

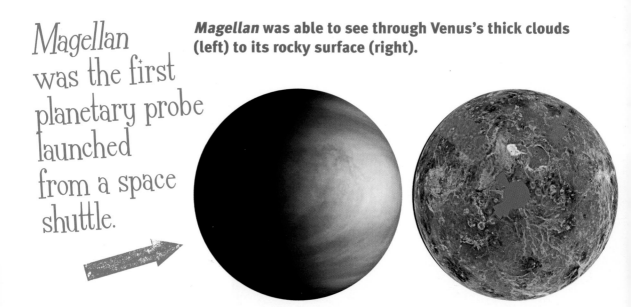

Landing on Mars

Mariner 4 completed the first successful Mars mission. This flyby probe took the first pictures of another planet from space. *Mariner 9* was the first spacecraft to orbit another planet. It helped scientists select landing sites for future missions.

Vikings 1 and *2* were designed to land on Mars's surface. These probes found evidence that water had once flowed on the planet. This showed scientists that Mars may have had the conditions necessary for life long ago.

Viking 1 took pictures of Mars's ice caps (visible at top), proving that frozen water existed on the planet.

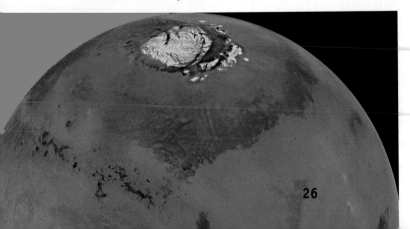

Each *Viking* probe had two parts: a lander and an orbiter.

Sojourner **inspects a rock on the surface of Mars that NASA scientists named Yogi.**

Roving on the Surface

By remote control, scientists drove the wheeled rover *Sojourner* over Mars's surface. *Sojourner* performed tests on rocks and measured temperature and wind. The twin rovers *Spirit* and *Opportunity* studied the planet's water and weather. From their data, scientists found even more evidence that Mars once had liquid water, rather than just frozen water, on the surface.

A newly developed sky crane system used cables and rockets to gently land *Curiosity* on Mars.

Curiosity was launched in 2011. The size of a large car, it landed in the Gale Crater on Mars in August 2012. First, *Curiosity* burned through Mars's atmosphere, protected inside a capsule. A parachute then slowed down the probe. Rockets helped adjust its position over the surface. Then wire cables lowered the probe gently onto the surface.

Curiosity has many instruments on board. It is fitted with 17 cameras. It will use a laser beam to break up pieces of rock. It will analyze the air. Its arm will scoop up soil and rock samples. The rover itself can do tests on these samples. The probe will look for the chemicals in the air and soil that show life may have existed there once. This mission will also help us think about how future exploration will be possible by more probes or by people.

The Chemistry and Camera, or ChemCam, instrument fires *Curiosity*'s laser.

NASA Probe Missions

Sun

Probe	Launch Date
Pioneer 6	1965
Pioneer 7	1966
Pioneer 8	1967
Pioneer 9	1968
Ulysses	1990
Genesis	2001

Mercury

Probe	Launch Date
Mariner 10	1973
MESSENGER	2004

Venus

Probe	Launch Date
Mariner 2	1962
Magellan	1989

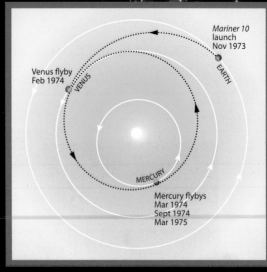

Mariner 10 launch Nov 1973

Venus flyby Feb 1974

VENUS

EARTH

MERCURY

Mercury flybys
Mar 1974
Sept 1974
Mar 1975

Path of *Mariner 10*

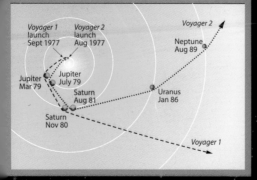

Paths of *Voyagers 1 and 2*

Mars

Probe	Launch Date
Mariner 4	1964
Mariner 9	1971
Viking 1	1975
Viking 2	1975
Sojourner	1996
Spirit/Opportunity	2003
Curiosity	2011

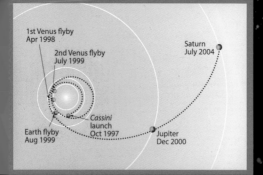

Path of *Cassini*

Outer Solar System

Probe	Launch Date
Pioneer 10	1972
Pioneer 11	1973
Voyager 1	1977
Voyager 2	1977
Galileo	1989
Cassini	1997
New Horizons	2006

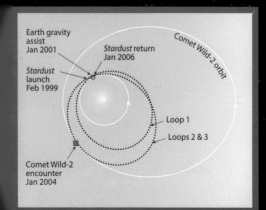

Path of *Stardust*

Comets

Probe	Launch Date
ICE	1978
Stardust	1999

Note: This is not a complete list. Visit the NASA Web site for a full list of probe missions.

Cassini learned new facts about Saturn's rings and magnetic field on its trip through the solar system.

CHAPTER 4

Exploring the Outer Solar System

Probes travel through space headed for a specific destination. But just because it is called "space" does not mean it's empty. The probes' equipment measures magnetic fields, space dust, and other data as they tour the solar system.

 Saturn takes almost 30 Earth years to orbit the sun.

Gas Giant Pioneers

While *Pioneers 6* to *9* headed toward the sun, *Pioneers 10* and *11* headed in the opposite direction. Both carry plaques with information about humans, in case they are ever found by living beings out in space. *Pioneer 10* was the first spacecraft to fly beyond Mars and through the asteroid belt that lies between the orbits of Mars and Jupiter.

Pioneer 10's trip from Earth to Jupiter took about nine months.

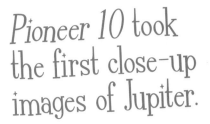

Pioneer 10 took the first close-up images of Jupiter.

As *Pioneer 10* passed by Jupiter, it transmitted hundreds of images of the planet and its many moons. *Pioneer 11* flew by Saturn and observed its rings and moons. After their missions were complete, both of the probes headed out of the solar system toward distant stars. They continued to collect and send back information as they traveled through space.

Voyagers

The flyby probes *Voyagers 1* and *2* took videos and recorded magnetic fields and atmospheric data of objects they passed. *Voyager 1* discovered rings and new moons around Jupiter and Saturn. *Voyager 2* continued on to Neptune and Uranus, where it found rings around both planets. On Uranus, it found a boiling ocean of water beneath the clouds. On Neptune, it observed an extremely windy atmosphere. Afterward, both probes continued out of the solar system.

Earth from Space

Sending probes to other planets has helped scientists learn more about our own planet as well. Some probes—such as *Galileo*, *NEAR Shoemaker*, *Stardust*, and *Deep Impact*—have used Earth as a gravity assist. While they flew by, they captured images of our own planet. These images give scientists a view of Earth from space.

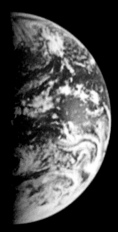

Orbiting the Giant Planets

Before *Galileo* reached Jupiter, it gave us new views of Venus and Earth. It flew close to the asteroids Gaspra and Ida, and photographed Comet Shoemaker-Levy 9 crashing into Jupiter's atmosphere.

Once in orbit, *Galileo* studied Jupiter and its moons. It observed the moon Io's active volcanoes.

It detected liquid water under the moon Europa's surface. This gave scientists hope of possible life there. *Galileo* also released a probe through Jupiter's atmosphere to collect data.

Galileo took this photograph of erupting volcanoes on Io.

Saturn's moon Tethys orbits near the planet's rings in this photograph from *Cassini*.

Cassini was the first spacecraft to orbit Saturn. One of its goals was to study Saturn's moons. *Cassini* carried an atmospheric probe, *Huygens*. *Huygens* was released into Titan's atmosphere and took pictures of the moon's muddy and rocky surface. *Cassini*'s images also showed **geysers** erupting from Enceladus's surface. Scientists didn't expect this from a moon they thought was frozen and still.

After passing Jupiter, *New Horizons* went into sleep mode for its eight-year trip to Pluto.

CHAPTER 5

The Journey Continues

The farther scientists want to explore, the farther probes will have to travel. It often takes probes years to reach beyond the inner solar system. *New Horizons*, a mission to study Pluto and the icy comets of the Kuiper Belt, was launched in 2006. It won't arrive there until 2015. When it finally reaches its destination, it may provide information to help scientists discover the origin of the solar system's water.

New Horizons will visit the Kuiper Belt, the possible origin of many comets.

New Tools

The *Deep Space 1* mission tested new engines and **navigation** software. The tests done with *Deep Space 1* proved that longer missions are possible.

The *International Cometary Explorer* (*ICE*) was the first spacecraft to fly past a comet. Following this, *Stardust* collected comet dust samples with a substance called Aerogel. Aerogel is like glass but much lighter because it is made mostly of air. It trapped thousands of particles from comet Wild 2.

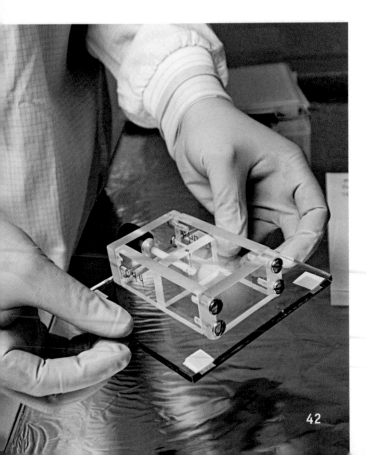

A NASA scientist holds a piece of Aerogel encased in plastic, containing samples of comet dust.

Future astronauts may one day visit places only machines could reach before, such as Mars, or even planets outside our solar system.

Eyes in the Sky

Probes allow scientists to go to places they cannot go to themselves. Scientists have been studying the data and images from probes. This has led to a better understanding of our sun, planets, and all the objects of our solar neighborhood. These missions also help us prepare to send humans to other planets.

The more scientists study, the more they can plan for the future and for the missions we can achieve in space. ★

First U.S. spacecraft: 1958, *Explorer 1*

First probe to use gravity assist: 1974, *Mariner 10*

First probe to study the sun's poles: 1994, *Ulysses*

First probe to send pictures of another planet from space: 1965, *Mariner 4*

First probe to orbit another planet: 1971, *Mariner 9*

First probe to be launched from a space shuttle: 1989, *Magellan*

First probe to fly beyond Mars: 1972, *Pioneer 10*

First probe to study Uranus and Neptune: 1986 (Uranus), 1989 (Neptune), *Voyager 2*

First probe to orbit a gas giant: 1995, *Galileo*

First probe to fly past a comet: 1985, *ICE*

Did you find the truth?

T Besides Earth, there is water in at least two other places in our solar system.

F No place in our solar system, other than Earth, could ever have supported life.

Resources

Books

Baker, David. *Probing Space*. New York: Weigl, 2010.

Jefferis, David. *Space Probes: Exploring Beyond Earth*. New York: Crabtree, 2009.

Scott, Elaine. *Space, Stars, and the Beginning of Time: What the Hubble Telescope Saw*. Boston: Clarion Books, 2011.

Visit the 100 Year Starship Web site at *100YSS.org* for more information on the challenges of travel to another star and ideas on how to solve them. You can also learn about the people who are trying to make the dream a reality!

Visit this Scholastic Web site for more information on journeying through our solar system:

★ www.factsfornow.scholastic.com

Enter the keywords **Journey Through Our Solar System**

Important Words

antennas (an-TEN-uhz) — devices that receive radio signals

atmosphere (AT-muhs-feer) — the mixture of gases that surrounds a planet

elliptical (i-LIP-tih-kul) — shaped like an oval

evidence (EV-i-duhns) — information and facts that help prove something is true or not true

geysers (GYE-zurz) — underground hot springs that shoot boiling water and steam into the air

navigation (nav-i-GAY-shuhn) — the act of finding where you are and where you need to go when you travel in a ship, an aircraft, or other vehicle

poles (POHLZ) — the geographical points that are farthest away from the equator

probes (PROHBZ) — devices used to explore space

radar (RAY-dar) — a way that ships, planes, or spacecraft find solid objects by reflecting radio waves off them and by receiving the reflected waves

revolve (ri-VAHLV) — to circle around something in a curved path

telescopes (TEL-uh-skopes) — instruments that make distant objects seem larger and closer

transmitting (trans-MIT-ing) — sending out radio signals

Index

Page numbers in **bold** indicate illustrations.

Aerogel, **42**
Aristarchus of Samos, 13, 14
asteroids, 7, 10, 14, 34, 38
atmosphere, **10**, 15, 17, 24, **25**, 28, 36, 38, 39

Cassini probe, **31**, **32**, **39**
comets, 7, **11**, 14, 31, 38, 41, **42**
Copernicus, Nicolaus, **12**, 13, 14

dwarf planets, 7, 9

Earth, **8**, **10**, 13, 14, 15, 16, 17, 18, 19, 23, **30**, **34**, **37**, 38

Galileo probe, **17**, 31, 37, **38**
gases, 9, 11, 18
Genesis probe, **23**, 30
geysers, 39
gravity, 7, **19**, 37
gravity assists, **19**, 37

International Cometary Explorer (*ICE*), 31, 42

Jupiter, **8**, 9, 14, **17**, **19**, **31**, 34–**35**, 36, 38

Kuiper Belt, 11, 41

landers, 17, 26

Magellan probe, **25**, 30
Mariner probes, 24, 25, 26, **30**, 31
Mars, **8**, **18**, **26**, **27–29**, 31, 34, **43**
Mercury, **8**, **24**, **30**
MESSENGER probe, **24**, 30

meteors, **10**
moons, 14, 17, 35, 36, **38**, **39**

National Aeronautics and Space Administration (NASA), **15**, 21, 22, 25, 27, 30–31, **42**
Neptune, **9**, 14, **31**, **36**
New Horizons probe, 31, **40**, 41

observatories, 14, 15
Oort Cloud, 11

Pioneer probes, **20**, 21, 22, 30, 31, **34–35**
Pluto, 9, 14, 18, **40**, 41

rocky planets, 8, 9, **25**
rovers, 17, **18**, **27–29**

Saturn, **9**, 14, **31**, **32**, 33, 35, 36, **39**
solar storms, **22**
Stardust probe, **31**, 37, **42**
sun, **6**, 7, 8, 10, 11, **12**, 13, **14**, **19**, **20**, 21, **22**, 23, 24, **30**

telescopes, **14**, **15**
timeline, **14–15**

Ulysses probe, **19**, 23, 30
Uranus, **9**, 14, **31**, 36

Venus, **8**, **20**, **25**, **30**, 38
Viking probes, **26**, 31
volcanoes, 24, **38**
Voyager probes, **31**, **36**

water, **26**, 27, 36, 38, 41

About the Authors

Dr. Mae Jemison is leading 100 Year Starship (100YSS). This is a new initiative to make human space travel to another star possible within the next 100 years. Dr. J is a medical doctor, engineer, and entrepreneur, or businessperson. She was a NASA astronaut and flew aboard the space shuttle *Endeavour* in 1992. She was the world's first woman of color in space. Dr. J was a college professor, author, and started several businesses. She also works to get more students involved in science. She started an international science camp for students called The Earth We Share. Dr. J enjoys dancing, gardening, and art. She lives in Houston and loves cats!

Dana Meachen Rau is the author of more than 300 books for children. A graduate of Trinity College in Hartford, Connecticut, she has written fiction and nonfiction titles, including early readers and books on science, history, cooking, and many other topics that interest her. Dana lives with her family in Burlington, Connecticut.